Dear ....,

You are invited to join us on a

VIP TOUR
OF THE
BOTANICAL GARDEN!

You will explore greenhouses and plant nurseries behind the scenes to discover everything that goes on to maintain this beautiful garden. You'll also access all areas to see horticulturists, garden designers, scientists, apprentices, students, and volunteers working hard to keep the garden running and making important discoveries that will help plants and fungi thrive across the world.

We look forward to welcoming you,

**The Botanical
Garden Crew**

Written by

Charlotte Guillain

W

WELBECK
EDITIONS

Illustrated by

Helen Shoesmith

Welcome to the Botanical Gardens

As you come through the turnstiles you can already see and smell colorful flower beds and hear the buzzing of bees. Many people are lining up to buy tickets for the botanical garden. Help yourself to a map—you'll need it to find your way around. There are volunteers here to answer questions and give people directions.

Let's begin the tour!

REFRESHMENTS

TOILETS

WELCOME ←

Contents

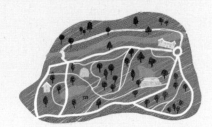

tulip
Tulipa

lavender
Lavendula

Flower Beds and Borders

Now your senses are being bombarded! You can see many bright flowers, smell their fragrance and the scents of herbs, and hear birds, insects, and other visitors. Long borders bursting with a wide variety of plant life stretch alongside the pathway.

These volunteer gardeners are busy weeding the borders. This is an important job that needs to be done every day to stop weeds from spreading and taking over the beds.

peony
Paeonia

A garden designer is working here to plan a new flower bed. She thinks about the various colors of plants that will grow together here and what patterns she can create. Opposite, or complementary, colors look best alongside each other, such as yellow and purple. She also thinks about the structure of the bed and includes plants that will grow to different heights and shapes.

What is pollination?

Pollination is one way that plants reproduce, or make more of themselves. Flowers contain pollen. When this pollen is taken to another flower of the same type, it fertilizes egg cells in the plant to make new seeds. Insects, animals, birds, humans, and even the wind can carry pollen from plant to plant to make this happen.

All of the plants here are labeled with their common name and scientific name. The scientific name is in Latin. It's used all over the world to make sure plants are labeled accurately in a way that everyone will recognize.

wallflower
Erysimum

wallflower
Erysimum

dog's tooth violet
*Erythronium
dens-canis*

The dark compost on the beds is called mulch. Mulch helps to stop weeds from growing and it keeps the soil moist, but not waterlogged. In winter it can also stop frost from damaging the plants. Mulch is made at the compost center, which you'll visit later!

The Palm House

The temperature rises to 82°F as you enter the palm house. Here you can see incredible plants from tropical rainforests around the world. Many of the plants are extremely valuable to people as sources of medicine or food. They grow fast and need to be cut back regularly to stop them from going through the roof!

This horticultural student is pruning a palm tree before it gets too heavy at the top. She needs to use a machine called a cherry picker to get high enough to cut the leaves off with a saw.

Climate change and rising temperatures around the world are making it harder for farmers to grow crops. In the palm house, scientists study plants that can grow well in hotter conditions. This gardener is harvesting cherries from a coffee species that grows better than other coffee plants where there is less rain. Scientists work with partners in other countries to test how the new species grows in different environments to find the best conditions.

arabica coffee
Coffea arabica

All the plants here need plenty of water, so the team spends a lot of time watering with long hoses. A mist is also sprayed around the plants to recreate the humid conditions found in a rainforest.

Scientists around the world are working to identify and protect plants that could be used to treat disease in humans. They work together to research the best ways to grow them and make medicines. For example, the Madagascar periwinkle could help to treat cancer and various trees can be used to treat malaria. The botanical garden does an important job of protecting and spreading endangered plants that might help us cure disease in the future.

mountain serdang
Livistone Speciosa

Madagascar periwinkle
Catharanthus roseus

The Waterlily House

You're in the hot and humid waterlily house now. This pond is full of enormous floating leaves! They're giant waterlilies, which were grown from seeds that came from the Amazon rainforest. The lily pads can grow to be 10 feet across. The pads are full of little pockets of air that make them float on the pond's surface.

Every year, new waterlilies are grown in the botanical garden, using seeds from the previous year's plants. They stay in the tropical nursery over the winter and are then moved to the pond in the greenhouse, where they grow very quickly!

This scientist is explaining how the waterlily's large, fragrant flowers open at night and only appear for 48 hours. They are white to start with, to attract insects for pollination. When their pollen has been released, the flowers turn pink.

It's important to keep the pond free of dead leaves and algae. The team has to get in the water once a week to clear it out!

These strange-shaped fruits dangling from the ceiling are gourds. They grow in tropical places, such as parts of Africa, where people cook and eat them.

In the wild, a beetle pollinates the flowers but here in the botanical garden a horticulturist hand-pollinates the waterlilies very early in the morning with a paintbrush. When the plant's fruit grows and ripens, he will come back to collect the seeds to grow more waterlilies.

This beautiful flower is a water lotus. Its incredible leaves are completely waterproof. If water droplets land on the surface, they instantly roll off, taking any dirt with them! The lotus needs the upper surface of its leaves to stay clean and dry to take in carbon dioxide and release oxygen so it can grow.

The Carnivorous Plant House

Welcome to the carnivorous plant house! These plants typically grow in places where there are very few nutrients in the soil, such as rocky or marshy areas. The plants attract and trap prey before digesting them to get the nitrogen they need to grow.

This is called a pitcher plant (*Nepenthes*) because part of it is shaped like a container or pitcher. When an insect is drawn to the plant's bright color and strong smell, it gets trapped in the liquid in the pitcher and can't climb out. The liquid contains a chemical that helps the plant digest the insect's decaying body. Yum!

Low's pitcher plant (*Nepenthes lowii*) attracts tree shrews, which feed on sweet liquid on the plant's lid. This causes the shrews to poop straight into the pitcher and the plant gets its nutrients from that!

pitcher Plant
Nepenthes

sundew
Drosera slackii

sun pitcher
Heliamphora

Many carnivorous plants also need insects for pollination, so their flowers grow far away from the pitcher traps.

Venus flytrap
Dionaea muscipula

purple pitcher plant
Sarracenia purpurea

The Venus fly trap (*Dionaea*) has three trigger hairs on the inside of its trap. If an insect lands on the plant and touches the hairs twice, the trap snaps shut within ten seconds around its prey.

trumpet pitcher plant
Sarracenia

THE FLYCATCHER BUSH (*Roridula dentata*)

This South African plant, the flycatcher bush, has sticky hairs all over its leaves, which attract insects. But this plant doesn't digest bugs for food! The stuck insects are spotted by the assassin bug, which is able to crawl over the plant and eat them. The assassin bug's poop is what the plant absorbs for nutrients.

The Tropical Plant Nursery

It's about to get hot and humid again now, because you're entering the tropical plant nursery. This huge greenhouse is split into several different climate zones. Almost 10,000 different plant types, or taxa, are grown for display in the greenhouses, for reintroduction in places where they are rare or extinct in the wild and for important research.

The temperature, light, and humidity in each zone of the tropical nursery are carefully controlled. If an area gets too much or too little sun or is too wet or dry, the computer responds and adjusts the conditions to suit the plants growing there. If things go wrong, an alarm goes off and a 24-hour response team springs into action to make sure the plants are protected.

WHAT IS PROPAGATION?

Propagation is growing new plants. Most gardeners can do this using seeds or cuttings from the leaves, stems, or roots of older plants. Horticulturists at the botanical garden use other techniques too, such as air layering. This is where a stem is still attached to a plant but grows its own roots. The stem can be separated and will then grow on its own.

Pest control is important in the nursery, so that insects don't destroy tender young plants. Ladybugs, wasps, and mites are used to help keep insects like aphids under control.

These amazing plants from South America are called bromeliads. They're sometimes called air plants because they don't have roots in the soil. Instead, their short roots attach them to trees, high in the forest canopy. They can't get water from the ground but their leaves are a funnel shape to collect the water they need to live and grow.

This *Uncarina* plant from Madagascar has pollen in sacs that attract beetles. When the beetles bite the sacs, the sacs burst and pollen squirts on to the beetle's head! The beetle then spreads the pollen when it moves on to the next flower, fertilizing it. The plant's fruit also sticks to lemurs' fur, so they spread them though the forest.

Lithops

Lithops

These little pebbles are actually a plant called *Lithops* from South Africa. Most of the leaf is underground, and its stone like disguise stops tortoises from eating it!

The Compost Center

You might be able to smell the compost center before you see it! Mulch is made here from natural waste and is used in the garden to feed plants so they grow well.

This is a delivery of horse poop, or manure. It has come from local stables, ready for the compost team to mix together with plant waste to make the mulch.

Fallen trees and cut-off branches are brought to the compost center and fed into a shredding machine to make wood chips. They are then mixed with grass cuttings and all the other shredded plant waste from the gardens and the horse manure.

The mixed mulch heap is steaming because it makes a lot of heat when the mixture reacts with water and the air. Microorganisms, such as fungi and bacteria, start to decompose, or break down, the waste in the pile.

The mulch heap is left at 140°F for three days to kill off any weed seeds so the gardeners won't spread these. The center of the heap is the hottest, so the team turns and mixes the pile regularly so all the waste material moves to the middle. It is usually fully decomposed and ready to use after around ten weeks.

A botanical horticulturist has come to fetch some mature mulch to spread on flower beds. The mulch is crumbly now and has stopped steaming so much. It also smells quite sweet by this stage! It will give the plants rich nutrients to help them grow and help them take in water. It also stops weeds from growing and can even prevent disease in plants.

The Fungarium

You're in the fungarium now. Like the herbarium, this is a place where specimens from all over the world are stored but these samples are all fungi. Scientists, students, research assistants, and artists are just some of the people who work here.

Fungi are not plants. They are more closely related to animals because they can't make their own food but get it from the world around them. Fungi make chemicals that kill other living things that might use resources they need. These chemicals can be useful for humans to make food and medicines, but they can also be poisonous! Fungi also have a very important relationship with plants, helping them to grow well.

There are millions of different types of fungi—many more than different kinds of plants. A mushroom that we see above the ground is just a small part of the fungus. Most of it is called mycelium and is found underground.

porcini
Boletus edulis

caterpillar fungus
Ophiocordyceps sinensis

death cap
Amanita phalloides

shaggy ink cap
Coprinus comatus

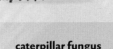

oyster mushroom
Pleurotus ostreatus

morel
Morchella esculenta

chicken of the woods
Laetiporus sulphureus

beefsteak fungus
Fistulina hepatica

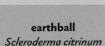
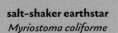
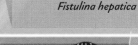

puffball
Lycoperdon

earthball
Scleroderma citrinum

salt-shaker earthstar
Myriostoma coliforme

fly agaric
Amanita muscaria

FUNGI

Mycologists are people who study fungi. When they find a fungus, they take photographs and record the details of its location before picking it and drying it out overnight. They also take tiny samples for scientists to look at in a laboratory.

NEVER PICK AND EAT FUNGI UNLESS AN EXPERT SAYS IT IS SAFE

zombie fungus
Ophiocordyceps unilateralis

This specimen shows a type of zombie fungus that invades insects. Tiny fungus spores floated through the air and settled inside this ant's exoskeleton. Then the fungus grew inside the ant until it burst out of its head. The fungus also makes the ant climb high in the trees so when it releases more spores they will be carried far by the wind.

The Science Laboratory

You'll need to put on a white coat now you're entering the laboratory. Scientists do some of the most important work at the botanical garden here. Their research will help people know which plants to grow in the future to beat disease and climate change.

This scientist is checking a plant extract that a company wants to use in a new shampoo. Her job is to make sure the plant ingredient they want to use matches the information the botanical garden has for that plant. In this way, she can make sure the company makes a product that is authentic and safe to use.

What is DNA?

DNA is a chemical found in all living things. It holds the specific information that each living thing needs to grow and reproduce. There are genes in DNA, which contain the information we use to identify different species and individuals. Scientists look at DNA to understand differences between plants and fungi and can identify them using just a tiny fragment.

Other research in the laboratory explores ways to protect bees and other pollinating insects. The scientists are learning about diseases that affect bees. They are discovering what can be done to help bees survive and continue pollinating the plants that so many living things need. Some plants have nectar and pollen that can protect bees from disease, so the team is finding out what these are and where they could be planted to help most.

The Seed Bank

Many botanical gardens have a seed bank to store seeds, but this one is extra special. To enter it, you head underground and go through a huge door like one you'd find in a bank vault. The vault is fire-, flood-, and bomb-proof to make sure the seeds are protected! The work done here is important for the whole world.

Partners all over the world collect the seeds of useful, rare, and threatened plants for the seed bank. Each seed is dried and cleaned, then an x-ray is taken to check the quality of the seeds, looking for bugs that may be inside the seeds. Scientists may also use a microscope to look at super-small seeds. Seeds are stored in jars well below freezing to keep them safe for years to come.

Over two billion seeds from all over the world are stored in this special seed bank and new seeds are added all the time. Some are from plants that are extinct in the wild, so the seeds offer a vital chance for people to reintroduce them. There may be seeds stored here that could become new foods or medicines for humans in the future.

WHAT IS GERMINATION?

Germination is when a seed starts to grow. It happens when the soil and amount of water and sunlight are just right. Germination means a root grows down into the soil and a sprout grows upward to become a stem and leaves.

Biologists can study and grow plants from the seeds in nurseries or special germination labs. They can try out new propagation techniques and transfer the new plants to greenhouses to discover the best conditions for them to grow. Seeds can be reintroduced to wild habitats all over the world when they are needed.

The Kitchen Garden

Go through a gate in the wall and you'll find yourself in the kitchen garden. This is where edible plants, such as fruits and vegetables, are grown. These plants are sold to the public, taken to the botanical garden's café, and also used for important scientific research.

This part of the garden has walls around it to keep out animals that might eat the plants. The walls also shelter the garden from wind and frost to protect the more delicate crops. The kitchen garden has a microclimate, which means it's a few degrees warmer than other parts of the botanical garden, so a wider range of plants can grow here.

apple
Malus domestica

turnip
Brassica rapa

radish
Raphanus
sativus

spring onion
Allium
fistulosum

lettuce
Lactuca sativa

peas
Pisum sativum

The kitchen garden helps us learn about edible plants that grow well in difficult conditions. As the world's climate changes, many crops that people have depended on are struggling with disease and hot temperatures. The team here experiments with different varieties of fruits and vegetables to see which ones are most resilient.

These are a type of vegetable called a tuber. Potatoes are also tubers but they can be damaged by disease caused by a fungus, called blight. More unusual tubers, such as oca and mashua from South America, are more resistant to blight and so could be a common food for us in the future. You can eat the roots and the leaves, which are delicious!

mashua
Tropaeolum tuberosum

oca
Oxalis tuberosa

potato
Solanum tuberosum

The Conservation Meadow

The garden opens up now as you step into the conservation meadow. This field is full of wild flowers and grasses, many of which are endangered in the wild. The colorful, sweet-scented flowers attract plenty of insects, such as bees and butterflies.

There are far fewer wild meadows now than there used to be. This means many wild plants are endangered or have disappeared. The conservation meadow team collects these seeds and then plants them here to conserve different species. They can then help to bring them back from extinction by reintroducing them in wild places.

The propagation supervisor is busy gathering seeds in the meadow to prepare them to be grown in the wild. Some seeds have a tough outer coating which would be worn down by harsh weather in their natural conditions. To get them to grow in a plant nursery, the propagation supervisor will need to wear down the seed covering with sandpaper or a sharp knife, so water can get inside and start germination.

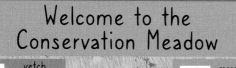

Welcome to the Conservation Meadow

vetch
(*Vicia species*)

ragged robin
(*Silene flos-cuculi*)

cuckoo flower
(*Cardamine pratensis*)

cowslip
(*Primula veris*)

In the wild, many animals live and feed in wildflower meadows. As well as insects, birds such as goldfinches feed on flower seeds and skylarks make their nests hidden away in the long grass. Mammals, such as mice, voles, and hares, also make the meadow their home.

A gentle buzzing sound tells you that bees are nearby. These bees are vital pollinators that keep the meadow healthy and help us to grow food crops. The conservation team have made sure there are a variety of wild flowers here to attract the bees and give them the nectar they feed on. The wild habitats that bees need have been reduced by humans building and using land for farming. The conservation meadow can give us all ideas about how we can help bees to survive.

The Children's Garden

It's time to relax and explore now in the children's garden. This is a place where children and families can play and learn about plants and what they need to grow.

This specialist teacher is telling a class on a school trip about pollination and the importance of insects, especially bees. He's showing them the different parts of a flowering plant and explaining what they are for.

Scientists and gardeners sort and organize plants into different groups. This sorting is called classification. Here, an explainer is showing a group of children how various plants in the garden are classified. They're looking at the plants carefully to spot similarities and differences.

Moving around in green, natural spaces is important for all of us to feel happy and healthy. The children's garden has lots of places to explore and play so the younger visitors here can have lots of fun!

There are fruits and vegetables growing in the children's garden too. Visitors can learn how to grow some of the plants we love to eat and can help to pick crops that are ready to eat. They may even get to taste some!

These young children are searching for minibeasts in the garden with magnifying glasses. They're learning how insects and other bugs need plants for food and how plants need them to reproduce.

carrot
Daucus carota

strawberry
Fragaria ananassa

cabbage
Brassica oleracea

The Café

Exploring the botanic garden will have made you hungry! Here in the café, you can eat lots of delicious food that was grown and harvested in the kitchen garden.

Because lots of the food in the café was grown in the garden, it's all seasonal. This means the fruits, vegetables, and herbs are all fresh and have grown naturally at the best time of year. None of the food has had to travel a long way, so it tastes delicious and is good for the environment.

There might be some food in the café that you haven't seen or tried before. Some of the fruits and vegetables are heirloom varieties, which means they are a type of plant that used to be grown a lot but isn't seen much today. Growing these plants now means we will have a wider variety of crops that cope better with disease in the future.

SPECIALS

There is also foraged, wild food on the menu in the café. This means that horticulturists in the botanical garden have picked wild herbs and plants, such as wild garlic, for the chefs to use. The teams working in different parts of the garden know when these wild plants taste their best.

The important scientific research done at the botanical garden means that some of the food on your plate in the café today might be what we all eat much more of in the future.

Exit Through the Gift Shop

You've explored most of the botanical garden now. On your way out, you can pay a visit to the gift shop and choose a plant of your own to take home!

Think about the space you have at home for a plant. Do you have a garden or a window box? Do you want to grow colorful flowers or some fruit, vegetables, or herbs? You might only have room for a house plant that you can grow indoors. You'll need to choose a place with plenty of light where it's easy for you to water your plant.

It's time to leave the botanical garden now. Which amazing plant, fungus, or scientific discovery will you be telling your friends about when you get home?